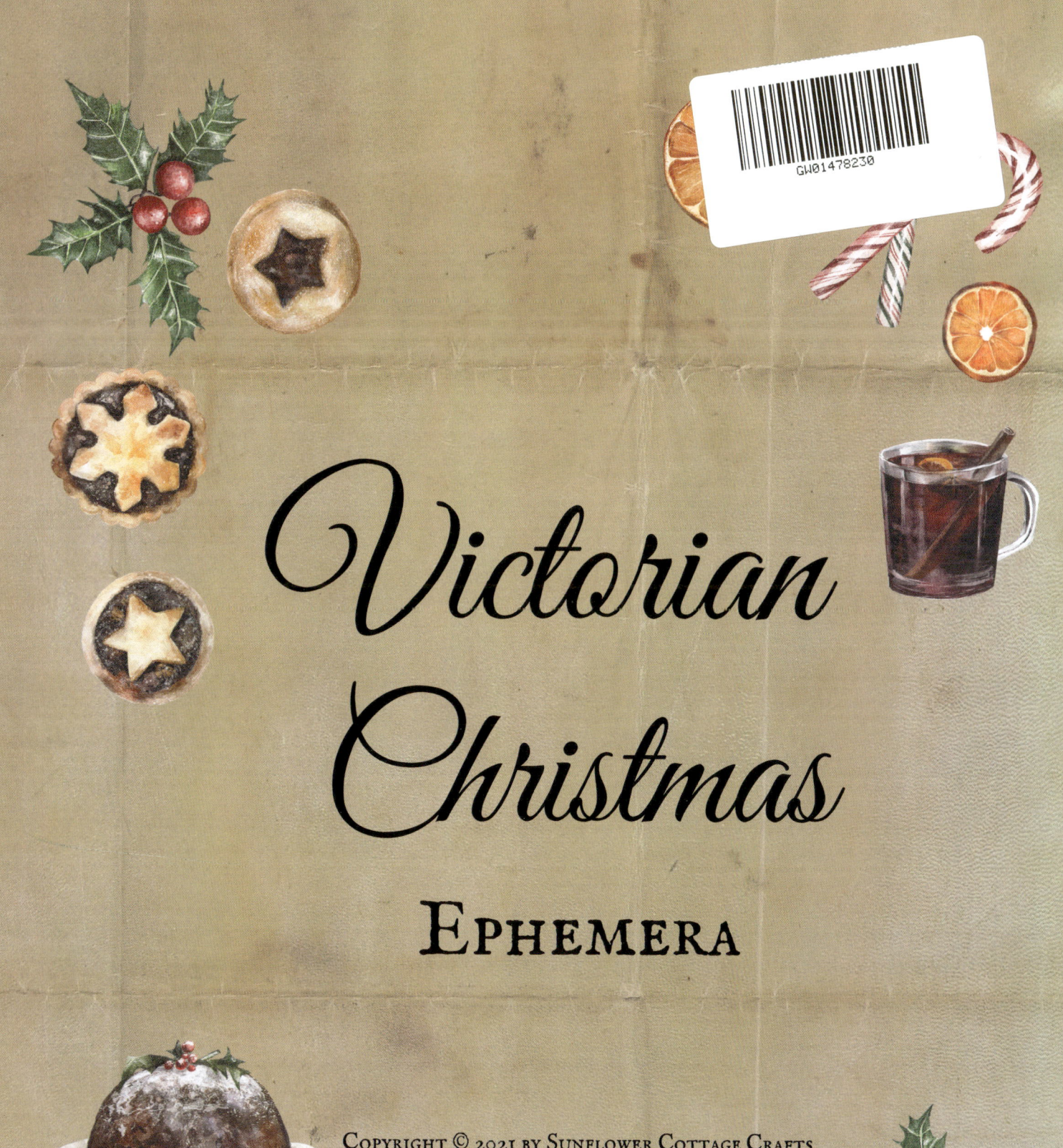

Victorian Christmas

Ephemera

Copyright © 2021 by Sunflower Cottage Crafts
All rights reserved. No part of this book may be reproduced or used in any manner without the written permission of the copyright owner except for the use of quotations in a book review.

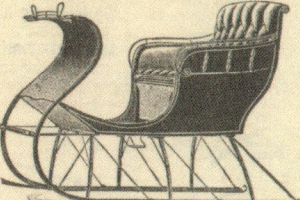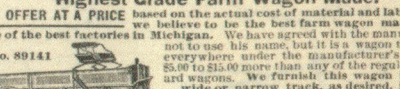

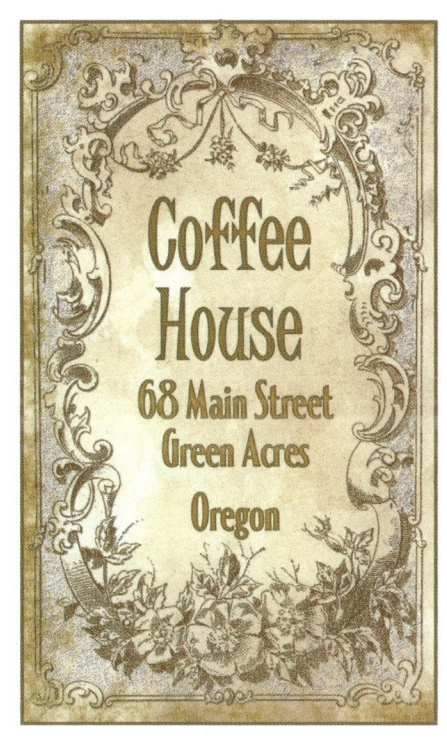

HOPE **LOVE**

JOY

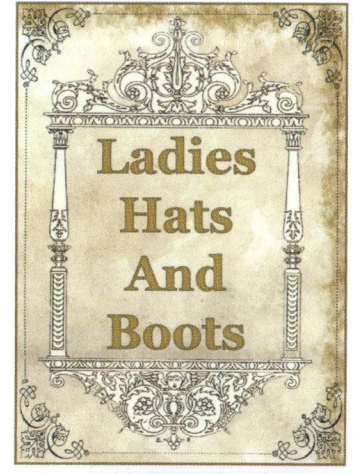

He saw that she was an Atalanta on ice as on turf.

The Coming of Father Christ

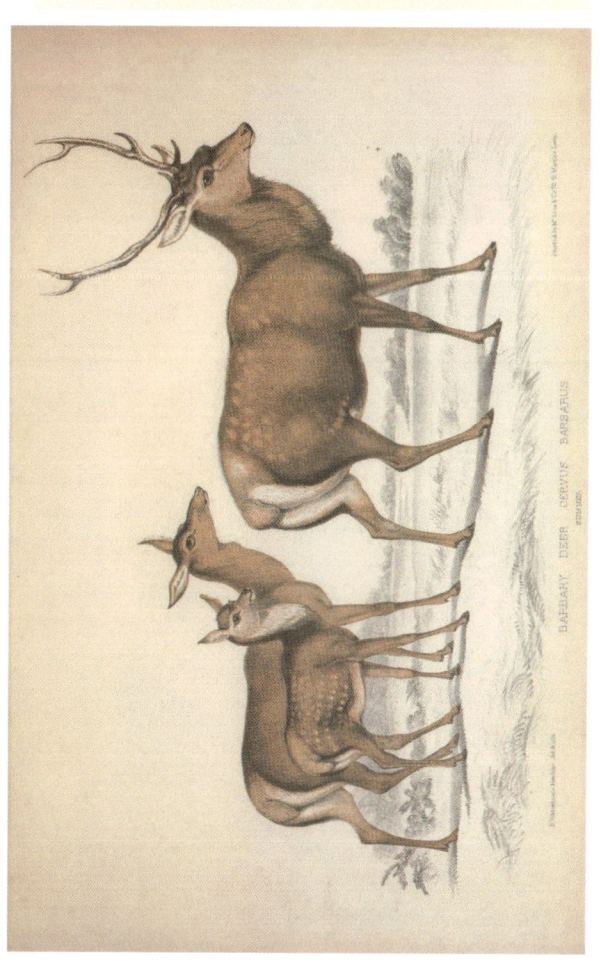

He determined on trying if he could not out-do Mrs. Tait.

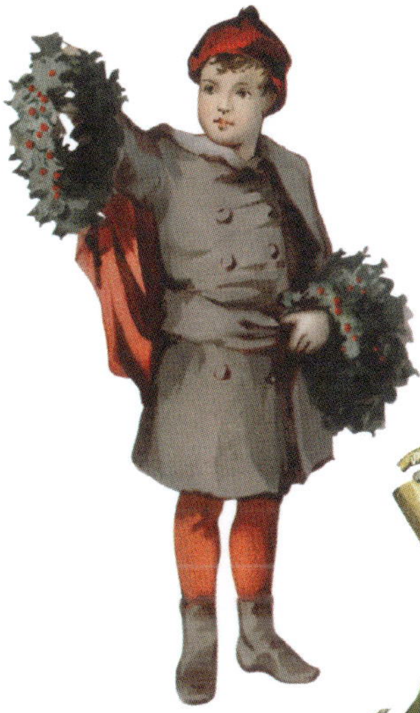

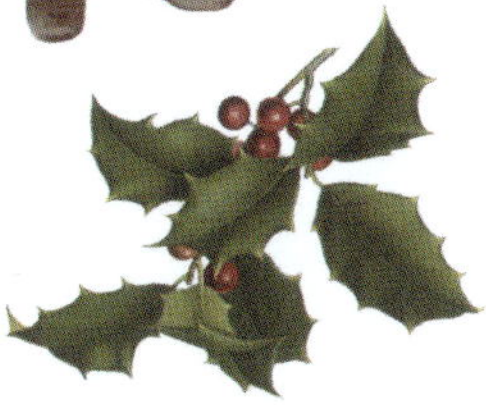

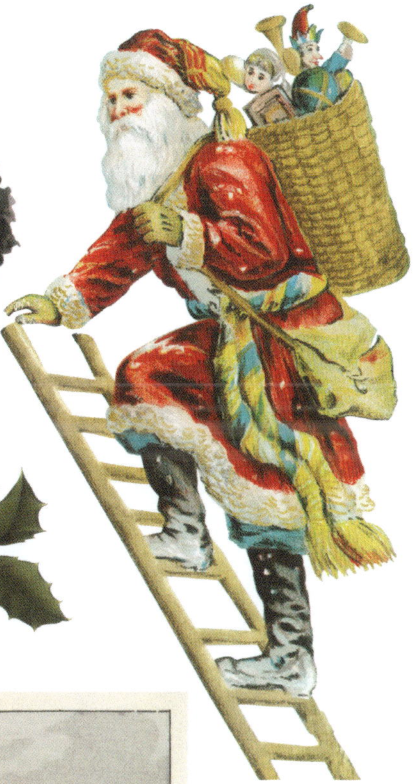

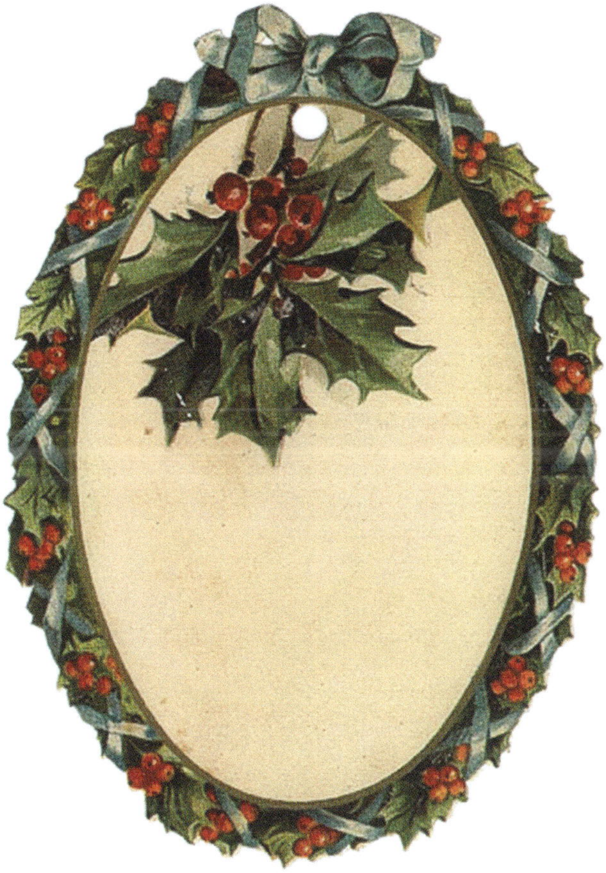

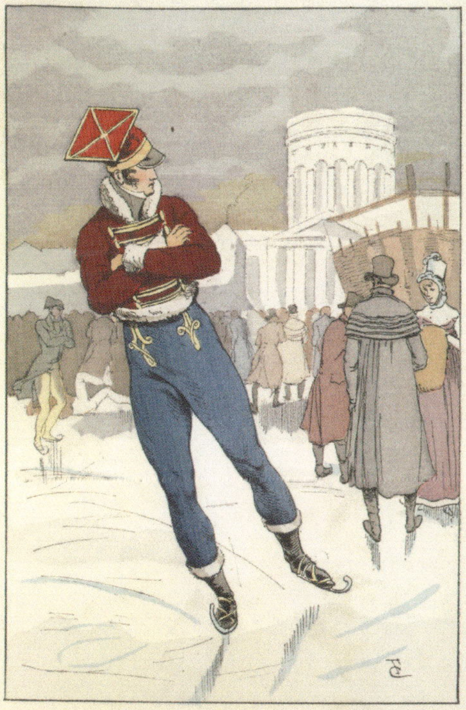

SKATERS ON THE RESERVOIR AT LA VILLETTE
(1813).

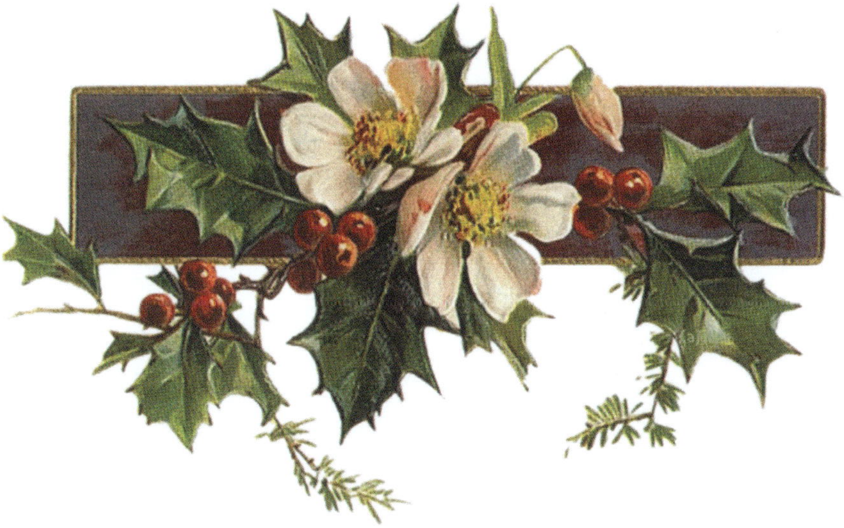

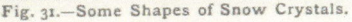

Fig. 31.—Some Shapes of Snow Crystals.

A Merry Christmas

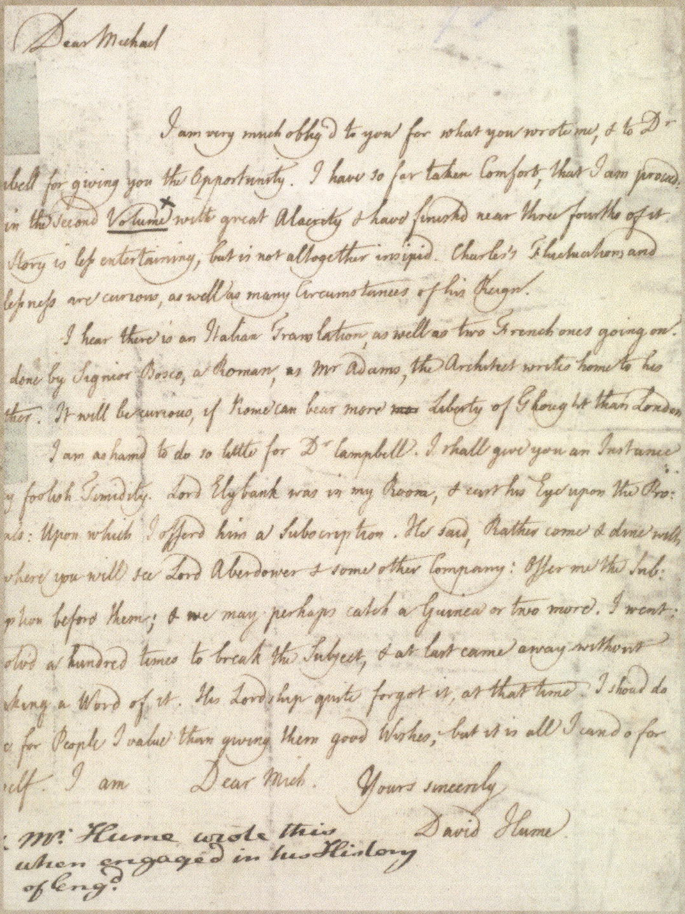

Dear Michael

I am very much oblig'd to you for what you wrote me, & to Dr
bell for giving you the Opportunity. I have so far taken Comfort, that I am proce
in the Second Volume with great Alacrity & have finish'd near three fourths of it
story is less entertaining, but is not altogether insipid. Charles's fluctuations, and
ness are curious, as well as many circumstances of his Reign.

I hear there is an Italian Translation as well as two French ones going on
done by Signior Bosco, a Roman, as Mr Adams, the Archives writes home to his
ter. It will be curious, if Rome can bear more liberty of Glowing than London

I am ashamd to do so little for Dr Campbell. I shall give you an Instance
foolish Timidity. Lord Elibank was in my Room, & cast his Eye upon the Pro:
als: Upon which I offerd him a Subscription. He said, Rather come & dine with
where you will see Lord Aberdower & some other company: Offer me the Sub:
ption before them; & we may perhaps catch a Guinea or two more. I went
lvd a hundred times to break the Subject, & at last came away without
king a Word of it. His Lordship quite forgot is, at that time. I shoud do
for People I value their giving them good Wishes; but it is all I can do for
lf. I am Dear Mich. Yours sincerely

David Hume

Mr Hume wrote this
when engaged in his History
of Eng.

Tea Shop

THE OLD BAKERY

Christmas Greetings

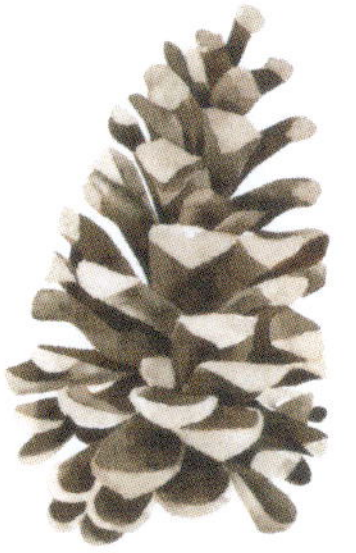

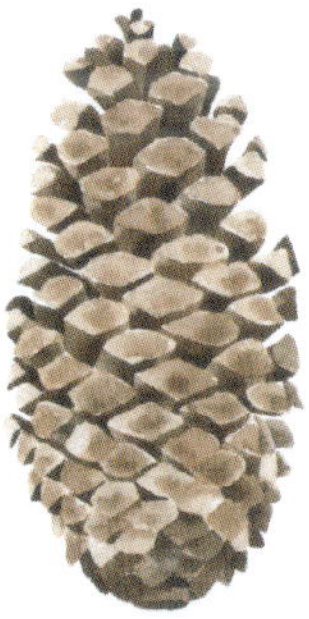

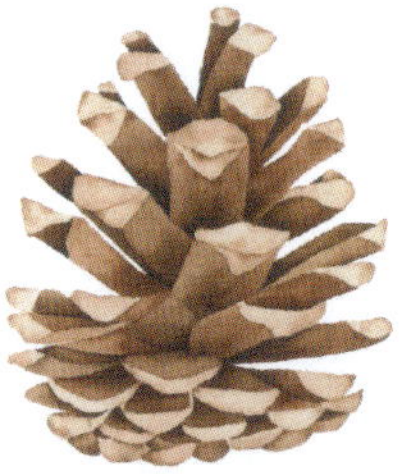

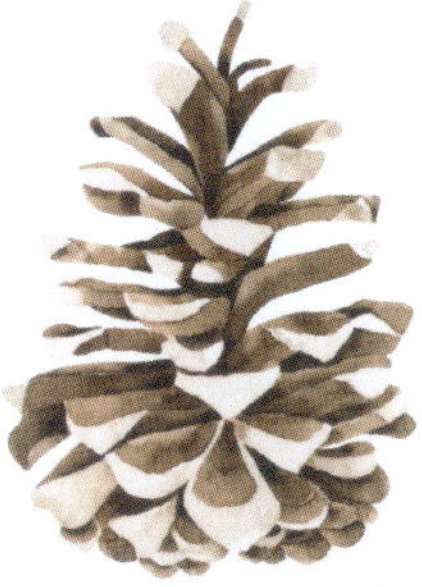

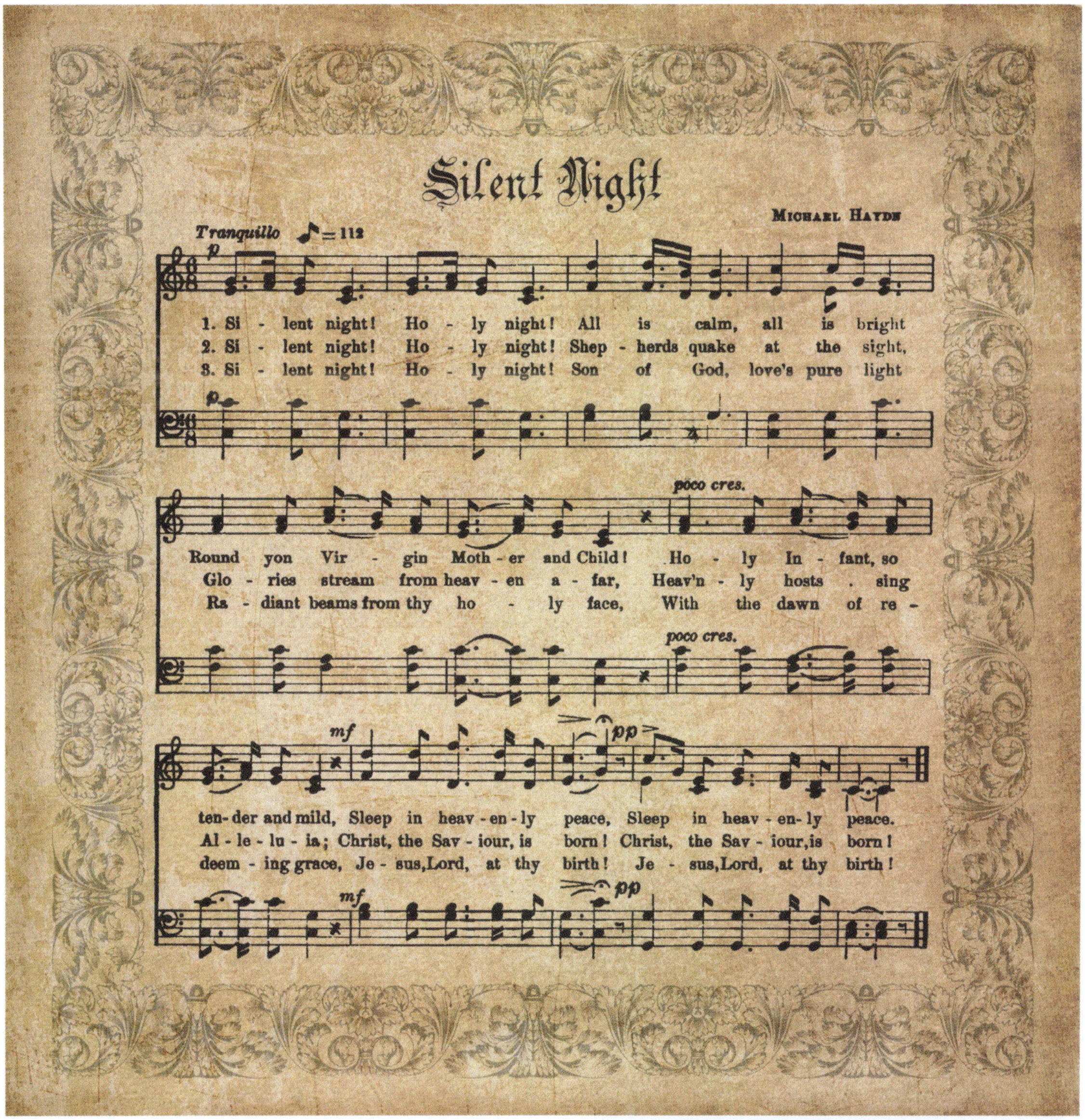

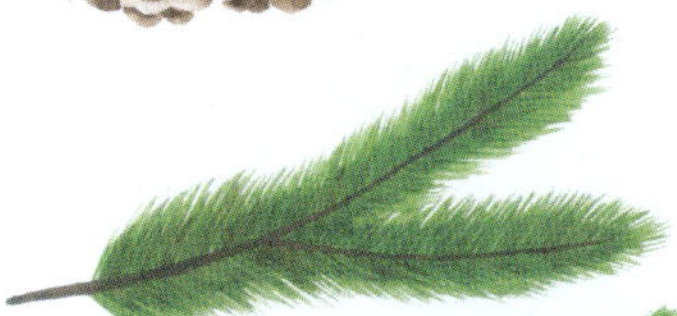

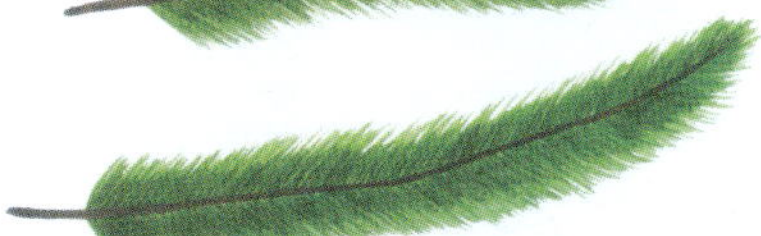

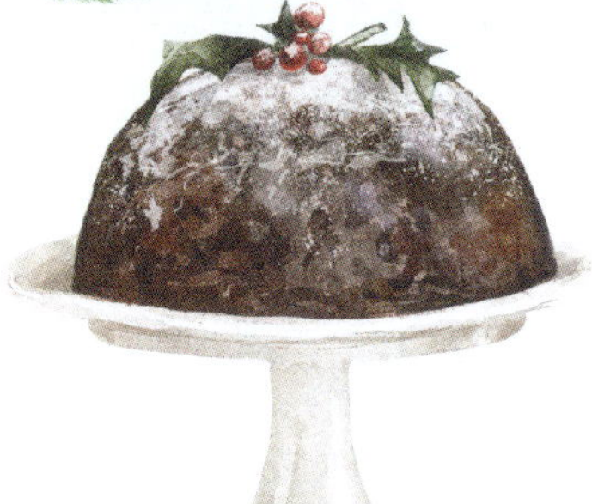

He saw that she was an Atalanta on ice as on turf.

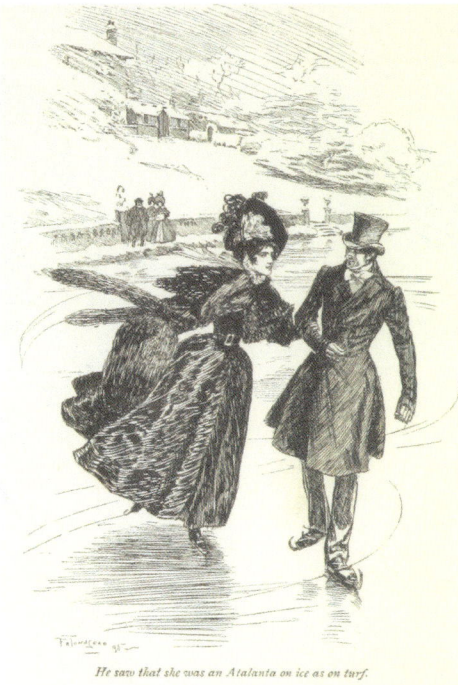

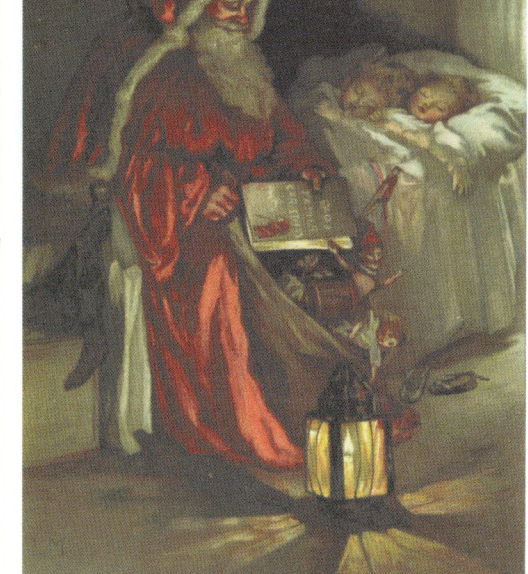

CONTENTS.

STAVE ONE.
Marley's Ghost 11

STAVE TWO.
The First of the Three Spirits . . 34

STAVE THREE.
The Second of the Three Spirits . . 56

STAVE FOUR.
The Last of the Spirits . . . 84

STAVE FIVE.
The End of it 103

A CHRISTMAS CAROL

Printed in Dunstable, United Kingdom

72511844R00025